To Terry

Do something wonderful!

Have fun!

Dee Ross

December 15, 1988

HAWAII

Published by Gallery Books
A Division of W H Smith Publishers Inc.
112 Madison Avenue
New York, New York 10016

Produced by
Bison Books Corp.
15 Sherwood Place
Greenwich, CT 06830

ISBN 0-8317-6826-6

Printed in Hong Kong

1 2 3 4 5 6 7 8 9 10

TEXT

DESIGN

JOYCE WALKER

MIKE ROSE

GALLERY BOOKS
An imprint of W.H. Smith Publishers Inc.
112 Madison Avenue
New York, New York 10016

A Bison Book

To Karen Chapman

Acknowledgements

The author and publisher of this
book wish to thank the following
people for their help: Elizabeth
Montgomery, who edited it, and Jean
Martin for the picture research.

Photo Credits

Bear Photo/Joe Carini: 20, 24, 25, 26, 30, 31, 36, 40, 47,
   55, 77 bottom, 81, 96, 97, 107, 123, 128
Camera Hawaii, Inc: 16, 45, 52
   Donna Martel/Camera Hawaii Inc: 21, Errol de Silva/
   Camera Hawaii Inc: 33, Werner Stoy/Camera Hawaii Inc:
   46, 53, 54, 74, 103, 118
Jeff Gnass: 1, 15, 18-19, 22-23, 28-29, 32, 34-35, 38-39, 41,
   42-43, 44, 49, 54-55, 60-61, 65, 69, 72-73, 75, 84-85,
   86-87, 88-89, 90, 91, 93, 98-99, 108, 114, 115, 119, 122
Hawaii Visitors Bureau: 17
Allan Seiden: 27, 50-51, 58, 71, 77 top, 83, 92, 94-95, 100,
   101, 104-105, 106, 109, 111, 112, 116 top, 117, 120, 121
Jim Shives: 68, 80, 110, 116 bottom
Jerry Sieve: 37, 56, 57, 59, 62-63, 64, 67, 70, 76, 78, 79,
   113, 124, 125 both, 120 127

3-6 Waikiki Beach and Diamond Head at dusk.
Photo © Greg Vaughn.

INTRODUCTION

There are echoes of the beginning of the earth itself in Hawaii's origins, a geologic narrative that is so extraordinary it seems like a legend. Fire, water, earth and sky all contributed to the creation of this archipelego. The story of Hawaii begins eons ago when a shuddering rift in the Pacific sea floor set the ocean into a fury, and pushed molten lava and ash upward through its crevasse. The lava hardened, the earth quieted, time passed, then once again subterranean pressure forced magma through the funnels created by hardened lava. For hundreds of thousands of years this intermittent activity continued until the volcanic mountains reached 13,000 feet to the water's surface, where they sent up vast clouds of steam, smoke and cinders, growing ever higher until they towered above the shining Pacific. Four of the peaks never reached the water's surface, and lie submerged west of the Big Island. Others merged together to become one island.

Wind, rain and sea worked their transforming magic on this strange and barren land, lashing lava rocks into sand and earth, and gentle slopes into steep cliffs. Life was slow to come to these specks of land with 2400 miles of water east and 3800 miles of water west lying between them and the continents. But finally come it did, borne as seeds or insects carried by wind currents or a wayward bird, or washed up on drifting wood. Flora and fauna flourished in this tropical paradise, where rich volcanic soil, temperate climate and sweet rains cultivated and evolved new species. Where the islands sloped gently into the sea, creating new habitats in the shallows, masses of lime-producing sea creatures set to work creating reefs that hardened into underwater barriers.

Descendants of Hawaii's first settlers depicted the isles' creation in no less fantastic terms when they explained that the sky was home of the God of Light and Mother of the Gods, whose firstborn dropped into the sea to become the island of Hawaii. She had also borne Maui and Kahoolawe when Mother of the Gods returned to Tahiti. In her absence the God of Light fathered Lanai by one woman and Molokai by another. When the angry Mother of the Gods returned she bore Oahu to another. Kauai and the rest of the islands were then spawned when the gods reunited.

The ancestors of the people who generated this legend had discovered the remote Hawaiian islands about AD 700. Motivated perhaps by a hostile conqueror or by a lack of natural resources, carrying their pagan religion, a multitude of plants and animals, and food and water, the adventurers left Micronesia and sailed north. Their 100-foot-long double-hulled canoes could each carry almost 100 people, and although their faith in the gods and in the birds they had seen flying southward helped sustain them, by the time they sighted land—more than 2000 miles later—even the most determined of them must have felt doubtful. When their incredible voyage came to an end and they cautiously ventured onto the shore, their destiny and that of the Hawaiian islands would be forever altered and intertwined. Naming the peaceful isles after their ancestors' fabled homeland, the Polynesian settlers built homes and cultivated gardens, some eventually returning to Micronesia to lead more people to the islands.

Although they became fiercer and their culture more restrictive by the arrival of conquering chiefs from Tahiti several centuries later, the Hawaiians had established a peaceful way of life, abiding by a worldview which deified nature, including the volcanoes, whom they believed were given life by the fire goddess Pele. The unforgiving *kapu*, or taboo, system regulated much of their daily life, banning women from touching many food delicacies or anyone from sitting or standing above a chief. The chiefs, or *aliis*, were men or women who inherited their rank, and were advised by the *kahunas*, those specialized in supervising the building of *heiaus* or temples, the making of canoes, healing and foretelling the future. Farming and fishing yielded an easy subsistence to the Hawaiians, who paid tribute to the *aliis* in fish nets, feathers and other goods.

About 40 years after Captain Cook visited the islands, and was killed in a scuffle there in 1779, Hawaii's great warrior king came to power. King Kamehameha, 'The Lonely One,' unified the islands by 1810, mainly by force, then ruled wisely and firmly until his death in 1819. His successor and son Liholiho had not been king long when he struck down the repressive *kapa* system, creating social disarray that worked to the advantage of the missionaries who arrived in the islands shortly after.

Landing in Hawaii in 1820 after an arduous five-month trip from Boston around Cape Horn, the missionaries were appalled by the free and easy manner of the natives. Men wore only loincloths and women wore skirts of *kapa*, or bark cloth, and loose mantles about their shoulders. Fond of music and gambling, the easy-going Hawaiians were converted and educated by the Protestant missionaries, led by the stern Reverand Hiram Bingham. Roman Catholic, then Morman, missionaries also arrived, printing presses were set up, schools were built and the Bible was translated, but as the *haoles*, or whites, gained foot-holds in the islands and transformed the culture, the native population succumbed to new diseases to which they had no immunity. Liholiho died in England from measles in 1824, typifying the fate of his people, whose numbers plunged from about 300,000 to 40,000 in the 100 years following their first contact with the white man.

Whalers used Honolulu and Lahaina, Maui, as their central ports of call, replenishing supplies and reveling in the generosity of the Hawaiian women. Corruption and venereal disease inevitably followed, staking the missionaries and whalers at odds in vying for influence among the natives. Seeking to affirm independence and establish order, Hawaiian royalty would write one constitution, then another. International competition for this prize in the Pacific spurred America to put the islands under secret protection in 1851, and as the century wore on Honolulu boomed into a modern-day city, sugar cane, coffee, rice and cattle made their way into the local economy, and waves of Chinese and Japanese laborers were imported to do the field work which the Hawaiians deplored. When King Kalakaua failed to force a return to Hawaiian customs, including respect for the absolute power of the monarchy, the stage was set for the future. His successor, Queen Liliuokalani, would be deposed in the bloodless revolution of 1893, given impetus by the trade interests of Hawaii's growing business, and a provisional government led by Sanford B Dole, of pineapple fame, would assume the helm. An era was at an end as Hawaii, as a territory of the US, turned her face toward a new century.

Dubbed by Mark Twain 'the loveliest fleet of islands that lies anchored in any ocean,' Hawaii developed and grew in the early 1900s, trying but always failing to gain statehood. With the bombing of Pearl Harbor in World War II, the territory gained international prominence. Racist voices were quieted by the performance of the Hawaiian Japanese Americans in this war, who distinguished themselves at Anzio and Cassino. On 21 August 1959, President Eisenhower signed the proclamation of Hawaiian statehood.

Hawaii's colorful past reveals itself in every aspect of its culture, especially in the interracial mix of its population. Proud of its early success with integration, which is more a way of life than an issue, Hawaii's more than one million people form a cultural mosaic, blending Caucasian, Hawaiian, Japanese, Filipino, Chinese, Samoan and others. Hawaii's eight main islands comprise a land that is at once Polynesian and American, a state with a mixed identity that lends it depth and character. Azure water lapping palm-fringed beaches, a field of orchids nodding with dew, the raucous din of a Waikiki nightclub, the sulfurous air in a seething volcanic crater—Hawaii presents a thousand moving images, but it is more than the sum of its parts. The islands' identity can be glimpsed, however fleetingly, in the shapes a hand traces in the air during a *hula* dance, or in the laughter of Hawaiian children playing in the surf.

OAHU

'I saw on the one side a frame-work of tall, precipitous mountains close at hand, clad in refreshing green, and cleft by deep, cool chasm-like valleys—and in front the grand sweep of the ocean: a brilliant, transparent green near the shore, bound and bordered by a long white line of foamy spray dashing against the reef, and further out the dead blue water of the deep sea, flecked with "white caps" and in the far horizon a single, lonely sail—a mere accent-mark to emphasize a slumberous calm and a solitude that were without sound or limit. When the sun sank down— the one intruder from other realms and persistent in suggestions of them—it was tranced luxury to sit in the perfumed air and forget that there was any world but these enchanted islands....'

Mark Twain wrote these words upon his first visit to Oahu in 1866, when he fell immediately under the spell of the islands with all their beauty and simplicity. Today, not only do virtually all visitors to Hawaii make their first stop in Oahu, arriving in the metropolis of Honolulu, but 80 percent of the state's population lives here as well. Tempered by a warm Polynesian sensuality and alive with the energy of youth and enterprise, Oahu's 617 square miles encompass both the cosmopolitan state capital and fertile plains lined with mountain ranges. Two separate volcanoes rose from the ocean floor and joined to form the two mountain ranges, Koolau and Waianae, that mark much of the island's terrain. The plains foster sugar cane and pineapple fields, dotted with plantation towns, private farms and suburbs. With the Pearl Harbor naval base, the military is a force in Oahu.

Hawaii's most familiar landscape—that of the famed Waikiki Beach backed by Honolulu's skyscrapers and curving along the sea to the eroded crater of Diamond Head—is located on Oahu's southern shore. Here architecture combines occidental, Oriental and Polynesian styles, just as the city inhabitants themselves reflect their international origins. A living past gleams in the moonrise over Waikiki and pulsates in the beat of the rhythmic *kalaau* sticks, as the city comes alive with the dances of a dozen different cultures. East and west harmonize colorfully on this beautiful island, where something is always happening. Palm trees trace their graceful lines in a sunset sky, lion dancers whirl and leap in Chinatown, a lighthouse blinks its solitary warning over the black sea, a *haole* rides his first wave on the surfboard, workers scurry along the docks to secure a towering cruise ship, and an outrigger canoe skims silently through the ocean surf. Oahu—the hub of Hawaii—keeps its own pace.

15. Palms are silhouetted at sunset in Honolulu's Aina Moana State Recreation Area.

16 The harbor at Honolulu is as crowded with pleasure boats as Waikiki is with resort buildings. This aerial view of Hawaii's best-known site shows the strip of Honolulu waterfront that ends at Diamond Head, a long-extinct volcano.

17 A rainbow arches over downtown Honolulu.

18-19 The moon rises over Waikiki at dusk, bathing Honolulu's buildings in twilight.

20 An outrigger canoe skims into Honolulu's harbor. Polynesians paddled in such canoes 2000 miles to settle the Hawaiian islands more than 1000 years ago.

21 A bicyclist pedals along a ridge above the city of Honolulu, which stretches below him to the sea.

22-23 Office buildings tower above Bishop Square in Honolulu.

24 Children from the Honolulu Community Center pose gleefully. Racial integration has long been the norm in Hawaii, where Chinese, Japanese, Hawaiians, Caucasians, Filipinos and Samoans comprise the majority of the population.

25 Wearing a leaf skirt and adorned with flowers, a Hawaiian performs the ancient hula dance, in which gestures and facial expressions tell a story.

26 The traditional lion dance, performed during the Narcissus Festival, celebrates the Chinese New Year. Honolulu's Chinatown is a fascinating blend of Chinese restaurants and herb shops, tattoo parlors and Oriental dry goods shops.

27 A Hawaiian performs the daring and entrancing fire dance.

28-29 Waikiki's night lights are reflected in the Ala Wai Canal.

30 Colorful leis, fashioned from many species of Hawaiian flowers, form a fragrant tapestry as they await sale.

31 Framed by a rice paper parasol, a Chinese woman smiles her greeting.

32 Fishing boats in Honolulu's Kewalo Basin. Sport fishing is fantastic in Hawaii; the annual Billfish Tournament attracts teams representing many foreign nations each summer.

33 Colorful spinnakers catch the afternoon light in the waters off Diamond Head.

34-35 At Honolulu the Keehi Boat Harbor's tranquil waters reflect the masts of moored sailboats at sunset.

36 Makapuu Lighthouse on Oahu's eastern tip overlooks Kaohikaipu Island and the larger Manana, or Rabbit Island, which is inhabited by birds as well as hares.

37 Boys feed fish in the crystal clear waters of Hanauma Bay, near Koko Head.

38-39 Pedestrians stroll along the walkway while bathers wade in Hanauma Bay and sunworshippers pursue a glorious Hawaiian tan in Koko Head Regional Park.

40 An impressive cruise ship docked at Honolulu testifies to the popularity of a Hawaiian vacation; more than four million people visit this state each year.

41 Sunbathers enjoy a blissful afternoon on Waikiki Beach.

42-43 Waves wash sand and rocks smooth at western Oahu's Kaena Point, with the Waianae Range receding into dusk.

44 Morning light bathes the ridges and valley of the Ko'olau Range, viewed from Nu'uanu Pali State Park.

45 A field of pineapples ripening in the sun near Haleiwa in northern Oahu. Carpeting the fields in green and gold, these succulent fruits flourish in the red volcanic earth of the island's valleys.

46 The Hawaiians originally taught the haoles, or whites, how to surf, and the haoles have been doing it ever since. Hawaii, the surfers' paradise, offers spectacular waves of up to 40 feet, and annual international competition.

47 *The grace and speed of the outrigger canoe is conveyed in this view of a team paddling out to sea.*

MAUI

The island of Maui is named after the hero-god whose many exploits enliven Hawaiian mythology. Maui is said to have brought the precious gift of fire, pulled up the Hawaiian islands from the sea, pushed the sky upward and captured the sun to force it to move more slowly across the sky. Maui achieved this last exploit standing on the crater rim of Haleakala, the island's 10,000-foot-high volcano—hence the crater's epithet, 'House of the Sun.' Maui is perhaps best-known for this other world above its clouds; no one who has ever seen the place can forget the vast crater floor stretching almost 3000 feet below the rim, its 21-mile circumference encompassing a moonscape of cinder cones ranging in color from grey to violet, red to green. Extremes coexist in Haleakala, which also contains forest, meadow, desert and a lake. Jack London described the House of the Sun as 'a scene of vast bleakness and desolation, stern, forbidding, fascinating. We gazed down upon a place of fire and earthquake. The tie-ribs of the earth lay bare before us. It was a workshop of nature still cluttered with the raw beginnings of world-making.'

In contrast to the dizzying heights of Haleakala, much of Maui's topography is aptly described in its nickname, 'The Valley Isle.' Comprised of two volcanic peaks that have joined together and eroded into fertile sloping countryside, Maui's 729 square miles range from jungled valleys and steep bluffs to irrigated fields and rolling foothills. While Haleakala's slopes feature colorful gardens, fields dotted with grazing cattle, jacaranda trees colored with purple blossoms and the cool eucalyptus, southeastern Maui's rocky cliffs give way inland to mossy stone walls dividing both wilderness and farmland. West Maui's coast harbors the historic town of Lahaina, the residence of King Kamehameha after he conquered the island in 1790 in the bloody battle at the Iao Valley. Later, some of Hawaii's first missionaries established a community here, and whalers found the town a hospitable port. Whales still frequent the waters off Maui, and watching these mammals of the deep is a popular winter pastime.

The island's other towns reflect the island saying, *Maui no ka oi*, or 'Maui is the best.' From the busy port city of Kahului to the narrow streets of Wailuku, which combine historic and modern architecture, to peaceful Hana on Maui's eastern point, the island's towns reflect its people's unique character. *Maui no ka oi* comes to mind when watching a sunset mottled by golden clouds or listening to water slapping the sides of boats resting in a peaceful harbor.

49 Surf crashes on the Ke'anae Peninsula on Maui's beautiful and secluded eastern coast.

50-51 An aerial view of the luxurious Kaanapali Resort, located on Maui's northwest coast looking toward the nearby islands of Lanai and Molokai. The condominiums and hotels of this complex offer 3000 rooms, and the resort's pools, shops, restaurants, golf courses and beaches keep guests busy.

52 The sun rises over Hana Bay. Hana, on Maui's easternmost point, maintains the spirit of old Hawaii in its distinctive Polynesian flavor, and its valley of waterfalls surrounded by tropical trees and flowers growing in lush profusion.

53 Sky and sea take on the golden hues of sunset at Kaanapali.

54-55 The waters of Lahaina, once frequented by whaling ships, now harbor many lovely pleasure boats.

*56 & 57 The windward coast of Maui is pierced
by rugged volcanic rocks.*

58 A giant bronze Buddha, imported from Japan, presides over Jodo Mission's Buddhist Cultural Park in Lahaina. The park commemorates Hawaii's earliest immigrants.

59 A mossy stone wall and abandoned shack blend into the dense forest near Hana Highway on Maui's northeast side.

60-61 Sunrise glows in the crater of Haleakala, Maui's 10,023-foot volcano which last erupted about 1790, leaving a crater encompassing 19 square miles.

62-63 Evening falls at Haleakala — The House of the Sun. Because of its unique geology, the rainforests of Haleakala National Park contain very rare native plants and bird species.

64 Colorful croton grows amidst volcanic boulders in the lush Iao Valley.

65 Silverswords at sunset on Haleakala. These exotic plants grow only on Maui.

KAUAI

Kauai, known as the Garden Island because its heavy, life-giving rainfall has created a lush tropical paradise of its fields and slopes, derives its name from the Hawaiian phrase meaning 'the fountainhead of many waters from on high and bubbling up from below.' Formed by the ancient volcano of Mount Waialeale, Kauai's 548 square miles comprise Hawaii's oldest and most north-western island. Steeped in legend and lush with verdant beauty, Kauai was home to the mythical Menehune, dwarf men who, it is said, worked only at night to create Kauai's dams, paths, temples and fish ponds. One explanation of the origins of the Mehehune legend points to the Tahitian equivalent of the name, which means 'commoner,' and alleges that when Tahitian chiefs came to Kauai around 1250, the 'little man' had to bear the brunt of their restrictive customs. The Maniniholo Dry Cave near Haena was said to have been dug by Menehune who were searching for the evil spirit who had stolen their fish. The fire goddess Pele also bore caves in Kauai, searching for a home, but moved on to occupy craters on other islands.

Kauai, the only island not conquered by King Kamehameha, submitted to all-island rule in 1810. A few years later Kauai's King Kaumaulii was almost induced to put the island under Russian protection; remains of a Russian fort at Waimea Bay attest to this chapter in history. The island at which the Polynesians, then Captain Cook, then the missionaries first landed, Kauai's history is indeed a colorful one.

Partially ringed by King's Highway, along which the sacred *alii* were once carried, Kauai's landscape is a mosaic of plantation towns, fields of taro and sugar cane, wild canyons and gulches, sheer cliffs, jungled valleys, peaceful beaches and sparkling rivers. Journalist Clifford Gessler described Kauai as 'a maze of worn peaks, striped canyons, and gulches cutting long low fields and rippling with cane, and tree-dotted upland pastures sloping to the misty mass of the great central mountain, Waialeale, long thought to be the wettest place on earth.' Magnificent Waimea Canyon, frequented by rainbows and metamorphosizing with the changing light of day, cuts gorges 3000 feet deep into western Kauai. Jagged, untamed cliffs, visited only via helicopter, airplane or boat, tower above the ocean along the Na Pali coast. The awe-inspiring green vertical folds of the Kalalau Valley remain unchanged from the days when they harbored Koolau the leper, who hid here to evade exile to Molokai.

Kauai's wilderness contains the *iliau* tree and the *mokihana* berry—found only on this island—as well as wild orchids, guavas, ti, poinsettias, bougainvilla, flowering vines, plumeria and a fragrant collection of other tropical flora. Rich in history and swathed in the mists of legend, beautiful Kauai makes its unique contribution to the lore of Hawaii.

67 Reefs give way to a palm-lined shoreline on Kauai's untamed Na Pali coast.

68 *A sea cave on the Na Pali coast. Stretching for 20 miles along northwest Kauai, this wilderness playground offers ribbon waterfalls, deep valleys, rugged cliffs and secluded beaches.*

69 At sunset a geyser of seawater spumes into the air out of a lava tube — Kauai's Spouting Horn.

70 Crystal clear water laps at the shore of the idyllic Lumaha'i Beach on the north coast of Kauai.

71 A surfer pauses to evaluate the waves at Poipu Beach on Kauai's south shore.

72-73 A field of taro stretches across the floor of Hanalei Valley. Used for making poi, taro is cultivated but also grows wild all over the islands.

74 *Sugar cane tassels catch the afternoon sun
in the Kauai countryside.*

75 Sugar cane being harvested by crane. Plantation towns grew up in Kauai around the sugar industry, and many of the fields now grow papaya, guava and macadamia nuts.

76 *The silver cataracts of Opaekaa Falls make a pleasing contrast to the lush greenery of its setting on the eastern side of the island.*

77 *Two of the many orchid varieties cultivated on the islands. The dainty and colorful flowers are used for making leis and for shipping to the mainland.*

78 *Latania grows at the edge of Waimea Canyon. The magnificent ridges and folds of this 2857-foot-deep gorge stretch north from Kauai's southwest coast, and harbor such rarities as the iliau tree, found only on Kauai.*

79 *A tropical pool in Olu Pua Gardens grows thick with waterlilies and harbors umbrella plants on its banks. Located near Kalaheo, Olu Pua — meaning 'floral serenity' — is situated in 12 acres of rolling hills.*

80 *The folds and pinnacles of remote Kalalau Valley, on northwest Kauai, once provided refuge for the infamous Koolau the Leper, who lived here five years after evading the entire Hawaiian National Guard.*

81 The most effective way the view the isolated and spectacular Na Pali cliffs, rising up to 3000 feet from the sea, is by helicopter.

MOLOKAI AND LANAI

The Kalohi Channel divides Molokai and Lanai, the two smallest of Hawaii's six major islands, which lie between Oahu and Maui. Less-visited and less developed than the other islands, Molokai and Lanai retain more of the old Hawaii in the wildness of their countryside and the character of their communities.

Shaped like a slipper, Molokai's 260 square miles support a population of almost 6000, over a third of whom live in the town of Kaunakakai on the island's southern shore. The sounds and smells of a seaport permeate this town which resembles a western-style trading post, where the wharf is always busy. Most of Molokai's other towns lie east of Kaunakakai, along the southern and eastern shores. From here the land slopes upward to inland mountains topped by the 4970-foot Kamakou. Northeast of Kamakou spreads the fertile Halawa Valley, where Hawaiians fish and farm much as they did a century ago. Hawaiian lore surfaces at the silver cascade of nearby Moaula Falls, where swimming is advisable only if a ti leaf tossed into the pool floats; otherwise the *mo'o,* or lizard, dwelling below is restless.

Much of Molokai's northern Pali coast is a beautiful and practically inaccessible series of plunging cliffs. Midway across the island the green plateau of the Kalaupapa peninsula juts into the sea, backed by 2000 feet of steep cliffs. A place of exile for sufferers of leprosy from Hawaii's islands in the mid-nineteenth century, Kalaupapa today harbors a community of patients and release patients of the sickness which is today called Hansen's disease. Near Saint Philomena's Church a memorial commemorates the Belgian priest Father Damien, who lived here from 1873 to 1889, helping upgrade the community's quality of life until his own death from leprosy.

The pear-shaped island of Lanai can be easily seen from Molokai's southern shore. Formed by a single volcano, Lanai's 90,000 acres include 15,000 acres given over to pineapple cultivation. The plantation town of Lanai City, located in the center of the island, features lovely stands of Norfolk pines and the crisp air its altitude yields. In contrast to the lush golden, green and red fields of pines, much of Lanai's northwest is arid plateau, accessible by four-wheel drive vehicle only. This desert-like landscape of hard-packed red earth and scrubby vegetation ends abruptly to the west in cliffs which seem to fall away into the ocean.

On the remote northern shore of Lanai, lava rocks and sandy beaches are interspersed with abandoned ships and temporary shelters made from driftwood and salvaged materials. The desolation here speaks of Lanai's past, when the island was believed to be inhabited by evil spirits until Maui's King Kaalaneo banished his troublesome son, Laululaao, to Lanai. Laululaau rid the island of the spirits, and people settled here in the early 1400's. King Kamehameha enjoyed a resort on Lanai, which was later visited by Protestant and Mormon missionaries. In 1922 Lanai was bought by the Dole Company who built Lanai City, irrigated the land, put in roads and created the harbor from which hundreds of thousands of pineapples venture forth during the harvest season. Lanai, like Molokai, retains the flavor of its history in its enterprise and its unspoiled landscape.

83 Graceful palm trunks curve skyward in a Molokai coconut grove. Mark Twain described these trees as 'feather dusters hit by lightning.'

84-85 The ocean meets Molokai's coast of rock and sand at Puu o Kaiaka at sunset.

86-87 An aerial view of Molokai's Kalaupapa Peninsula, where sufferers of leprosy were exiled in the mid-nineteenth century.

88-89 Coconut palms reach into twilight at Onealii Beach on Molokai.

90 A desolate scene at Lanai's Shipwreck Beach, where a disintegrating hulk lies in the Kaholi Channel between Lanai and Molokai.

91 The sea washes black rocks at Lanai's palm-fringed Hulopoe Beach.

92 Stretched across the warm beach sand at
Kaluakoi, sunbathers enjoy the beautiful Molokai
weather.

93 A motorboat plies the waters of Auau Channel, which runs between Lanai and Maui.

94-95 Carrying tourists on a spectacular guided tour, sure-footed mules pick their way up a steep ridge from Kalaupapa.

96 A giraffe in the Molokai Ranch Wildlife Park
is not shy about accepting handouts. This
800-acre privately-owned preserve also harbors
ostrich, Indian black buck, impala and oryx.

97 Untamed Lanai is best explored in a four-wheel-drive vehicle. A dirt track called Munro Trail leads to Lanaihale at the top of the island, from where almost all of Hawaii s major islands can be seen.

98-99 Weathered lava boulders in Lanai's Garden of the Gods seem like ruins of an ancient temple.

100 The simplicity of the church of Saint Philomena, or Father Damien's Chapel, in Kalawao, testifies to the purity of Father Damien's faith.

101 Father Damien's memorial in the cemetary alongside the church of Saint Philomena. The first white resident in the lepers' colony at Kalaupapa, Father Damien devoted his life to relieving the victims' suffering until his own death from the disease in 1889.

HAWAII

Known as 'the Big Island,' 'the Orchid Island' and 'the Volcano Island,' Hawaii is all three of these things. The largest Hawaiian island by far, Hawaii is comprised of five volcanic mountains, two of which reach a height of more than 13,500 feet from the surface of the sea. About 25 miles apart, the lofty peaks of Mauna Loa and Mauna Kea jut above the clouds. Although Mauna Kea has long been dormant, Mauna Loa to the south has erupted twice since 1950, and Kilauea on Mauna Loa's southeast slope has erupted dozens of times in the last decade.

In one of the first recorded observations of Kilauea, missionary William Ellis wrote in 1823, 'Astonishment and awe for some moments rendered us mute, and, like statues, we stood fixed to the spot, with our eyes riveted on the abyss below. Immediately before us yawned an immense gulf.... The bottom was covered with lava, and the southwest and northern parts of it were one vast flood of burning matter, in a state of terrific ebullition, rolling to and fro its ''fiery surge'' and flaming billows.' The fire goddess Pele is said to inhabit Kilauea's Halemaumau Crater. And it was into Kilauea that the Hawaiian woman Kapiolani defied taboo by climbing to the rim and tossing into the crater the sacred *ohelo* berries that women were not allowed to touch. The volcanoes, responsible for Hawaii's very existence, are central figures in Hawaiian mythology. The unique landscape they generate has evolved rare forms of flora and fauna which scientists carefully study.

In contrast to the wondrous land of the volcanoes, Hawaii's Kona coast features a balmy climate. The tourist, coffee and fishing industries thrive on this coast, which stretches 60 miles along Hawaii's western shore, and encompasses many landmarks in Hawaii's history. While King Kamehameha lived and made his plans for island unity at Kailua, the town was also the site of the sacred Ahuena *heiau* which was destroyed when King Kamehameha II abolished the taboo system. Missionaries built Kailua's Mokuaikaua Church of *ohia* wood and lava rock, while Hawaiian kings summered in the stately Hulihee Palace. Sixteen miles south along the coast is Kealakakua Bay where Captain James Cook was killed, and just south of here, at Honaunau, is the City of Refuge—a sanctuary at which fugitives gained absolution and immunity. Hawaiian history permeates the Kona coast as does air itself, described by Jack London as 'faintly balmy, fragrant and spicy; and cool, deliciously cool, a silken coolness, a winelike coolness—cool as only the mountain wind of Kona can be cool.'

Hawaii harbors a wealth of diverse landscapes and historic sites, from the large but friendly city of Hilo to tropical rain forests and fields of wildflowers. The essence of this varied island is found in the silvery colors of spray from a waterfall, the sight of a fishing boat motoring into the sunrise, the smells and sounds of delight at a sumptuous *luau,* and in the frozen ocean of lava stretching across a crater floor.

103 A boat makes its way seaward into the Kona sunset on the island of Hawaii.

104-105 A sudden squall washes over Kona, a village tucked between a blue-green bay and Mount Hualalai on Hawaii's western coast.

106 *The leisurely life is enjoyed by vacationers at a Kona village resort.*

*107 Adventurous boys take turns leaping from a
rock outcropping into the azure ocean below.*

108 & 109 With their fierce expressions, the Ki'i figures at the City of Refuge, or Pu'uhonua O Honaunau, guarded the pursued and the vanquished who found sanctuary in this ancient haven.

110 *A festive air surrounds the Hawaii Annual Wahine Fishing Tournament, as fish are displayed and measured.*

111 *A shopper browsing through the shells at an outdoor market in the Kona area.*

112 A swimmer walks into the foamy sea at the black sand beach of Kaimu, on Hawaii's eastern shore.

113 The shimmering volcanic sand is washed by a gentle surf. The black sand was formed when molten lava met the cold seawater and exploded into fragments.

114 *The tranquil setting of St Peter's Catholic Church at Kahaluu Bay was also the site of an ancient temple at which the Hawaiians placated their gods.*

115 *The colorful interior of the Painted Church,
or St Benedict's Catholic Church, blends biblical
and Hawaiian scenes.*

116 A worker picks vanda orchids and a woman
in a colorful muumuu teaches others how to make
a lei.

117 Preparing for the traditional Hawaiian luau,
a pig is filled with heated rocks, wrapped in leaves
and served with an abundance of every delicacy
imaginable, from avocadoes and coconut to sushi
and moray eel.

118 Flying above the Hamakua Coast reveals miles of sugarcane fields flourishing on the rich soil.

*119 Cattle pick their way through the rock-strewn
pasture. First brought to the islands in 1793, cattle
have been raised on the lush Hawaiian
grasslands ever since.*

120 Thirty thousand feet above the ocean floor, the snow-covered craters of Mauna Kea and Mauna Loa jut above the clouds.

121 The observatories atop Mauna Kea, operated
by the US, England, Canada and France, are the
world's highest astronomy site, situated above 40
percent of the earth's distorting atmosphere.

122 The smoking Halemaumau firepit lies within
Kilauea's vast crater.

123 Kilauea's recent eruption filled Halemaumau
with seething molten lava.

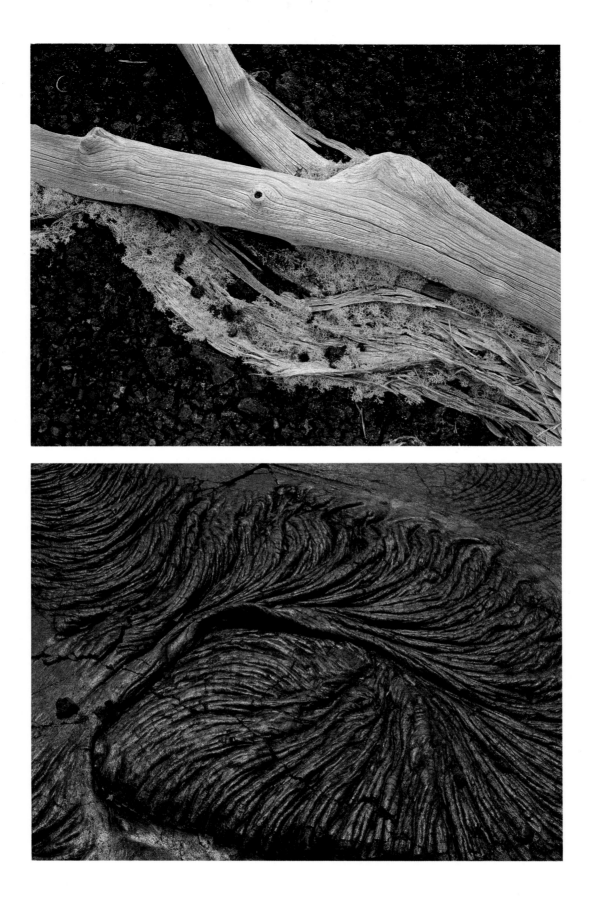

124 *Along Devastation Trail in the Kilauea Iki crater, the bleached remains of trees lie in a sea of volcanic rocks.*

125 top *The beginnings of life in the wake of destruction harken back to Hawaii's origins hundreds of thousands of years ago, when the sea floor rose in a series of eruptions to create the island chain.*

125 bottom *Ropey lava in Hawaii Volcanoes National Park, also called* pahoehoe.

126 Japanese Anemone and a tree fern branch create a lush picture in contrast to the bleak expanses of volcanic destruction in Hawaii Volcanoes National Park.

127 An angels trumpet tree grows near Rainbow Falls in Hilo's Wailuku River Park.